Legislative Assembly Arizona

Memorial and affidavits showing outrages perpetrated by

the Apache Indians

Legislative Assembly Arizona

Memorial and affidavits showing outrages perpetrated by the Apache Indians

ISBN/EAN: 9783337303440

Printed in Europe, USA, Canada, Australia, Japan

Cover: Foto ©ninafisch / pixelio.de

More available books at **www.hansebooks.com**

MEMORIAL AND AFFIDAVITS

SHOWING

OUTRAGES PERPETRATED

BY THE

APACHE INDIANS,

IN THE

TERRITORY OF ARIZONA,

FOR THE

YEARS 1869 AND 1870.

PUBLISHED BY AUTHORITY OF THE LEGISLATURE OF THE TERRITORY OF ARIZONA.

SAN FRANCISCO:

FRANCIS & VALENTINE, PRINTERS, 517 CLAY STREET.

1871.

INTRODUCTORY.

It is customary and generally considered to be to the interest of new countries, to conceal as far as possible the hardships and dangers necessarily incident to their first settlement, with a view of inviting immigration and capital as rapidly as possible, and thereby overcoming these obstructions.

Probably, but few countries on the face of the globe presents greater natural resources inviting to immigration and capital than the Territory of Arizona. Nearly every mountain is threaded with veins of gold, silver, copper, and lead. Large deposits of coal and salt of an excellent quality are found. Nearly every foot of the Territory is covered with nutritious grasses, and stock thrives the year round without shelter or prepared forage. Nearly every product that grows in the temperate or torrid zone can be grown here to perfection and in abundance. There are vast forests of excellent timber; the mountains and valleys are amply supplied with pure water; the climate is warm, genial, and healthful, equal to any on the American continent.

With all these natural advantages, the subtile Apaches have been so constant in their depredations and destructive of life, that nearly all of the early pioneers have already fallen by their hands, and every industry and enterprise has been paralyzed.

The recent order withdrawing from the Territory a considerable portion of the Federal troops has excited general alarm among its citizens. The Territory is covered with the ruins of cities and towns that were once undoubtedly inhabited by a people of industry and enterprise, and who cultivated vast fields, as is shown by the remains of large irrigating canals. That people have passed away, and no one knows who they were. The cause of their destruction was undoubtedly the ravages of the implacable Apache, and our people now begin to realize, that unless assistance is given them, that they only await a similar fate.

In view of these facts, much as we desire immigration and capital, it has been considered but justice and humanity to our people to place upon record the truth regarding the condition of affairs in this Territory, and to do this, the affidavits of a large number of reliable citizens and officers of United States army have been taken, confidently believing that, when these facts are known, the press, the people of the United States, and the Government will demand and aid in subduing our hostile foe, and thereby reclaim from the savage one of the most valuable portions of our public domain.

Resolution authorizing Legislative Committee to take Testimony.

Resolved, By the House of Representatives, the Council concurring, that a Committee of two from the House and one from the Council be appointed as Joint Committee to inquire into the condition of the Territory, depredations committed by Indians, the amounts of property captured and destroyed, and all particulars connected therewith, as requested by a petition for a memorial from the people of Arizona Territory, and that such Joint Committee have all necessary authority to compel witnesses to appear before them, to administer oaths, and to take all necessary testimony in connection with the suggestions of said petition, and report their joint action to their respective Houses at their earliest convenience.

Adopted in the House, January 25th, and Messrs. Thos. J. Bidwell and F. H. Goodwin appointed Committee on the part of the House.

Adopted in the Council, January 25th, and Mr. J. T. Alsop appointed Committee on the part of the Council.

INDIAN COMMITTEE ROOMS, }
Tucson, February 17th, 1871. }

To the Sixth Legislative Assembly of Arizona:

Your Committee, appointed to take testimony in regard to depredations committed by hostile Indians in this Territory, from January 1st, 1869, to the present time, herewith report and submit for the consideration of the Legislature, the evidence upon which this report is based.

Your Committee have adduced a large amount of evidence from reliable witnesses, proving that the Indians are *now* in actual hostility with the settlers of this Territory. We have to report that on account of the limited time allowed in which to take evidence, a greater part comes from Pima County, but we believe that all parts of the Territory have suffered alike. We find from the evidence presented that our citizens have been murdered on the highways and in their fields; that hundreds of thousands of dollars' worth of property have been taken off and destroyed, and that murders and robberies are almost of daily occurrence. We find that some of the most fertile portions of our Territory are being abandoned by the settlers, on account of the repeated and destructive raids of the Apache Indians. We find that the U. S. mails have been frequently captured by the Indians, and the mail carriers killed; stations upon mail routes have been attacked by the Indians and those in charge murdered and the stations destroyed.

To sum up the evidence, it is our opinion that during the year 1870 the Apache Indians have been and are *now* in more active hostility than at any time since the Territory has been under the American flag.

A digest of the evidence and a memorial to Congress is herewith submitted.

J. T. ALSOP,
Of the Council.

T. J. BIDWELL,
F. H. GOODWIN,
Of the House of Representatives.

MEMORIAL

ASKING PROTECTION FROM HOSTILE INDIANS.

To the Senate and House of Representatives of the United States, in Congress assembled :

Your memorialists, the Legislative Assembly of the Territory of Arizona, most respectfully submit to your honorable bodies, the following memorial, for the purpose of giving reliable information of the condition and necessities of the people of the Territory.

Your memorialists are aware that occupying a geographical position on the southwestern border of the United States, with no railroad or telegraph facilities and limited political influence, the suffering and deaths which have attended the settlement of this Territory, in consequence of the hostility of the Apache Indians, are but little known or appreciated beyond our borders. Your memorialists have therefore compiled testimony, by a large number of reliable citizens and officers of the army, with the view of fairly and more forcibly making known the condition of affairs in this Territory, which shows that a savage war still exists herein, causing the murder of hundreds of our citizens and the loss of a vast amount of property; and that at no period since the settlement of the Territory has the loss of life and property been greater than during the year 1870; and that the hostility of the Apache Indians, and want of protection, have led to the abandonment of many valuable mines; and that large farming settlements have been and are being abandoned for like causes. Your memorialists would further state, that the people of this Territory are attached to it, and find in its genial climate, pastoral, agricultural, and mineral resources, all the elements necessary to make it a populous and desirable country in which to live; that they have endured the hardships and braved the dangers incident to a pioneer life, with a fortitude that should command the admiration of a brave people; and though hundreds have fallen beneath the scalping knife and tomahawk, or suffered torture at the burning stake, the survivors fill the broken ranks, and continue the contest. Our people have made their homes here, and have no other, but unless protection be given them, the constant decimation that is made will soon sweep from the country all traces of civilization, except deserted fields and broken walls.

Your memorialists respectfully ask a careful consideration of the facts presented; and as faithful citizens of the United States, and your own kindred, and in the name of humanity, we ask for protection and assistance. Therefore, be it

Resolved, By the Council and House of Representatives of the Territory of Arizona, That our Delegate in Congress be, and he is hereby, requested to use all honorable means to bring this subject to the earnest and favorable consideration of Congress; and be it further

Resolved, That the Secretary be requested to transmit a copy of the foregoing memorial and resolutions to our Delegate in Congress.

AFFIDAVITS.

W. A. SMITH, *sworn:* He is a farmer and resides at the Cienega in Pima County, Arizona; has resided there for three years; that the Apache Indians have committed depredations at and near his farm, as follows, to-wit:

In January, 1869, the mail carrier's horse was shot from under him, and the U. S. mail taken and destroyed by the Indians.

In the spring of 1870 a U. S. soldier, named Bernard Hogan, was shot dead in the door of the house in which a picket guard was quartered.

In August, 1870, his house was attacked and two of the three inmates murdered—the witness only escaping by concealment; all the crops and everything destroyed about the premises.

WM. MORGAN, *sworn:* He is a farmer and resides at Sonoita Valley, Pima County, Arizona, and is a member of the present Legislature. The following depredations have been committed in his neighborhood by the Apache Indians, to-wit:

In May, 1869, E. G. and G. Pennington (father and son) were killed while plowing in their field, and all of the horses, mules, and other movable property belonging to the farm was taken.

In November, 1869, Benjamin Aikin and a Mexican (name unknown) were murdered while harvesting corn, and all their property taken.

The same year, Joaquin Tapia and Jas. Catterson were murdered while traveling on the road. Joseph Goldtree, who was traveling with them, escaped with his clothing riddled with bullet and arrow holes.

In the same year Thomas Vonday was murdered while standing in the door of his house and the house robbed.

In the same year, six U. S. soldiers were attacked by about sixty Indians, and one soldier killed.

In the same year, another attack was made on seven U. S. soldiers, and one of their number killed.

In June, 1870, David Holland was murdered in his field, a small boy made captive, and four horses taken. At the time of this occurrence there were seven more men in the field who escaped.

Also during the year 1870, Thomas Venable and two other men were murdered on the road from Tucson to Camp Crittenden; two wagon loads of goods and twelve mules were taken; that twenty-five U. S. soldiers and three citizens followed the Indians, overtook them and were repulsed.

Deponent lost, in 1870, nine head of cattle and two horses. Mr. Thomas Gardner, living at the same place, lost five cattle and two horses, and Mr. W. Cook two head of cattle : that all of the foregoing depredations were committed within twelve miles of Camp Crittenden; that the highways are unsafe, and if Camp Crittenden be broken up, the farmers will be compelled to abandon their farms.

ALBERT DECKER, *sworn :* Keeps a station at Gila Bend, in Arizona Territory; that in February, 1869, his herder was murdered by the Apache Indians.

In January, 1870, he lost four horses; followed them and recovered three from the Apache Indians.

In April, 1870, lost forty goats, thirteen sheep, and one yoke of oxen ; and in the same month eight mules and four horses were taken from his place, belonging to other parties—all by Apaches ; believes all the roads of this Territory dangerous to travel for small parties.

MICHAEL O'RILEY, *sworn*, and says that he keeps a station eighteen miles north of Tucson; that in August, 1870, the Apache Indians came in the afternoon within one-fourth of a mile of his house and took one fine horse and six mules.

That in the last of August, 1870, they shot a man in his employ named Bloom, and took one mule.

SAMUEL HUGHES *sworn*, and says he is a clerk and resides in Tucson; that he has personal knowledge of the following depredations by the Apache Indians, to-wit :

In November, 1869, they killed a Mexican near Camp McDowell ; in June, 1870, he with twenty-five others were attacked, twenty-two miles from Camp Grant, by about fifty Indians ; Newton Israel and Hugh Kennedy were killed; two wagons loaded with merchandise, and seven mules were taken at the same time; the bodies of the men were badly mutilated and one of them burned; that life and property are unsafe on the public roads.

WM. S. OREY, *sworn*, and says he is a farmer and resides at Tucson; has resided in this Territory fifteen years; that he has suffered from the Apache Indians during the last two years as follows:

In February, 1869, seven head of cattle taken; in March, 1869, nine head of cattle taken; in July, 1869, two head of cattle taken; in September, 1869, four head of cattle taken; in January, 1870, one horse and one cow; in March, 1870, three head of cattle; in May, 1870, four head of cattle; in July, 1870, five head of cattle; in November, 1870, three head of cattle — total loss, $2,000; that he does not consider life or property more safe than when he first came to the Territory; considers no road leading from Tucson safe; that if Camp Crittenden is abandoned the settlements of the Sonoita and Santa Cruz Valleys must be abandoned; that in 1869 the U. S. Government was furnished with grain at $2.49 in gold per one hundred pounds; that in 1870 for less than $3.00, and that flour is now worth $4.00 to $4.50 per one hundred pounds.

CHARLES A. SHIBEL, *sworn*, and says he resides at Tucson in this Territory; is Assistant Assessor of Internal Revenue; that the following depredations by the Apache Indians have come under his observation the past year:

In August, 1870, while coming from Camp Goodwin to Tucson, on the Rio Grande mail road, he found the mail coach destroyed and the following persons murdered and *mutilated:* John Collins, Wm. Burns, and two U. S. soldiers. They were *scalped*, one partially burned, and another with his eyes gouged out; and he believes this Territory is now in almost a defenseless condition.

JOSEPH GOLDTREE *sworn*, and says he is a merchant, and resides in Pima County, Arizona; that he in company with Joaquin Tapia and Jas. Catterton were attacked by twenty-one Apache Indians, between Tubac and Camp Crittenden, on the first day of January, 1869; his two companions were killed and his horses and carriage were taken; he was wounded and his clothes riddled with bullets; that he considers Indian outrages more frequent the past two years than ever before.

ISAAC GOLDBERG *sworn*, and says he is a merchant; that he has met with losses by the Apache Indians, during the past year, and had men in his employ killed, as follows: in March, 1870, Julian Grijalba killed between Camp McDowell and Phœnix, while carrying the United States mail—horse and mail taken; that his ox train was attacked and his wagon master, Angel Ortiz, was killed; that Paymaster Rob't Morrow, U. S. A., was attacked at the same time.

In August, 1870, he lost twelve yoke of oxen and six horses, making a total loss of property during the year of $2,150; that during the past two years he has furnished supplies to the U. S. Government at the following prices: hay, $13.36 per ton; beans, $4.49 per hundred pounds.

Considers the roads of the Territory extremely dangerous, and believes that the Indians are more hostile now than five years ago.

JOHN G. BOURKE *sworn*, and says he is 2d Lieutenant 3d Reg't U. S. Cavalry; has been in this Territory ten months. On May 28th, 1870, went with twenty U. S. soldiers to the relief of train that was attacked by Indians on the Camp Grant road, twenty-two miles from Camp Grant; found the burning ruins of two wagons, the dead body of a man named Israel, also a man named Kennedy, mortally wounded.

Three weeks afterwards a party of prospectors were attacked fifteen miles from Camp Grant, by about sixty Indians, capturing horses, wagon, provisions and all they had, and wounding three men.

Afterward, while scouting in the Apache Mountains, a man named Graff was killed while engaged in action with the Indians.

In September, 1870, while in pursuit of the Indians that captured the overland mail, he found two *skulls* that appeared to have been burned; also found a *scalp.*

October 1st, 1870, pursued Indians that had stolen stock from Tucson, and in an action with them had two men wounded.

Does not consider any of the roads that he has traveled safe, except in strong force.

HOWARD B. CUSHING, *sworn:* Is 1st Lieutenant 3d U. S. Cavalry.

(The testimony of Lieutenant Cushing is substantially the same as that of Lieutenant Bourke.)

FREDERICK MARSH, *sworn:* Resides eighteen miles from Tucson; is engaged in stock raising. Since January 1st, 1870, has met with the following losses, to-wit:

January, 1870, lost seventeen head of cattle; April and May, 1870, lost eight head of cattle; July, 1870, lost nine head of cattle; July, 1870, lost four head of horses; September, 1870, lost six head of cattle—making a total loss of $1,250;

And says that depredations are more frequent than two years ago, and that the roads are unsafe for small parties.

HENRY C. LONG, *sworn*, and says he resides at the "Tres Alamos," on the San Pedro River in this Territory; that depredations by Apache Indians have been perpetrated in his neighborhood as follows:

In July, 1869, three men were murdered—one named Johnson, one named McMurray, and the name of the third to him unknown.

In May, 1869, a man named Culver was murdered while plowing in his field.

In January, 1870, Samuel Brown and John F. Sims were murdered about three miles from his house.

In March, 1870, J. G. Jackson was murdered.

And that from January, 1869, to January, 1871, there has been stolen from the "Tres Alamos," by the Apache Indians, at least twenty-five head of stock, of the value of $2,000.

JAMES REILLY, *sworn*, and says he is 2d Lieutenant 21st U. S. Infantry; has resided in this Territory since July 10th, 1869, and has personal knowledge of the following depredations by the Apache Indians, viz.:

Saw a U. S. mail rider at Blue Water Station, who had been attacked by Indians and wounded.

October 9th, 1869, the U. S. mail coach was attacked at Dragoon Springs, and the following killed: Col. John F. Stone, the stage driver and an escort of four men of Co. D, 21st U. S. Infantry—all the U. S. mail and property taken or destroyed. Same month, two hundred head of cattle were taken near the same place.

November, 1869, the Government herd, thirty head of cattle and five mules, were taken at Camp Bowie.

February, 1870, at Camp Bowie, cut from the picket line and got away with two horses; same month, five mules were taken from same camp.

May, 1870, three horses were taken.

June, 1870, stage coach with U. S. mail was attacked at Stein's Peak, and one mule killed. Same month the mail carrier was attacked and his horse killed.

In August, 1870, the U. S. mail coach was taken on the road to Tucson, and four men murdered.

In December, 1870, Tully and Ochoa's train was attacked forty-five miles from Tucson.

Considers the Indians of this Territory exceedingly hostile, and considers small parties unsafe traveling through the country.

HENRY E. LACY, *sworn*, and says he has resided in this Territory about six years, four years of that time at Camp Goodwin; testifies to a number of depredations committed near that Post. Is of the opinion that the Apache Indian considers military posts, garrisoned by white troops, only for their own protection, and to feed them; that three-fourths of the Apache Indians that assume to be friendly, commit depredations upon the settlers and then return to their Post for safety.

MARIANO SAMANIAGO, *sworn*, and says he resides in Pima County, Arizona, and freighter by occupation. In December, 1870, hauled guns and ammunition to Camp Goodwin, and on December 28th, 1870, saw a part of said guns and ammunition issued to Apache Indians, at Camp Thomas, by a Sergeant; have also seen guns in possession of Apaches who claimed to have borrowed them from the commanding officer. He personally knows of scouting parties of Indians constantly absent from the reservation with hostile intent.

December 24th, 1870, was informed by Indians at Camp Thomas that a few days previous they had attacked a train near the Cienega de los Pimas, and killed one man and taken some stock. Col. Green informed me that he knew nothing of the affair only what the Indians informed him of.

In December, 1870, the Indians stole five mules from me at the reservation, and informed me that they had killed three and disposed of the other two.

Deponent knows that life and property is very insecure on all roads in this Territory.

IGNACIO VARELA, *sworn*, and says he is a farmer. In the spring of 1869 two men were attacked by Apache Indians and sought refuge in his house. The same day, his hired man was attacked while driving his team, killed the oxen and destroyed the other property; and about the same time, nine men were attacked, one of which was killed. Also mentions several other depredations during the same year. Also testifies to a number of depredations committed during the year 1870, near his place, including the destruction of his crops, and considers the Indians more hostile now than at any period heretofore.

JOHN B. ALLEN, *sworn*, and says he resides at Tucson, is a farmer, and the present Territorial Treasurer; that he has sold and delivered to the U. S. Government, during the year 1870, six thousand pounds of flour at $4.49 per one hundred pounds: that in January, 1870, the Apache Indians took from him thirty-three head of mules; in February, 1870, sixteen head of imported cattle, worth $2,300. During the same year several other depredations, and during the year a total loss of $6,750.

Considers the Apache Indians more hostile now than at any other period within six years.

C. W. C. ROWELL, *sworn*, and says he has resided in this Territory since 1863, and is at present U. S. District Attorney; testifies to Apache Indian depredations that have come under his personal observation as follows:

In April, 1869, James G. Sheldon was murdered four miles west of Camp Willow Grove, his horse killed, his gun and $300 in money taken.

On January 13th, 1871, the Yavapai Apaches captured twenty-nine head of his mules at Gila City, twenty-five miles from Fort Yuma; total value of said mules, $1,620.

L. E. BROWN, *sworn*, and says he is a farmer; has resided in this Territory since 1863.

In May, 1869, the Apache Indians attacked two U. S. Government teams, seven miles from Camp Crittenden, killing one U. S. soldier and wounding another, and captured ten mules.

That they burned Thomas Vonday, who was killed by them, nine miles from Camp Crittenden; also that they murdered Mr. Pennington and his son, in the Sonoita Valley, and captured property to the value of $1,000; also that they killed a cow at Camp Crittenden and stole some tents from the rear of the officers' quarters.

In November, 1870, Edmund and Pacheco's teams were attacked, eight miles from Camp Crittenden, and a portion of the train captured.

Also states that on account of the hostility of the Apache Indians, he has been compelled to abandon his farm in the Sonoita Valley, and that other settlers will be compelled to do the same.

JUAN ELIAS, *sworn:* Resides at Tucson, and testifies to the following depredations by hostile Apache Indians:

In April, 1869, the witness lost three horses, fifteen oxen, and five mules; on July 18th, 1869, three horses; on August 7th, 1869, two horses; on December 20th, 1869, two horses; June 20th, 1870, two horses; August 17th, 1870, one horse; October 13th, 1870, fourteen beef cattle; January 23d, 1871, eleven horses; and at other times, the dates of which cannot be remembered, at least forty head of stock cattle; that he knows it is not safe for farmers to work in their fields in the vicinity of Tucson and San Xavier without some one to guard them while at work. The Apache Indians are more hostile and successful now than ever before, on account of the superior arms and ammunition that they have.

Francisco Romero, *sworn:* Is a farmer, and native of Tucson; testifies to depredations committed by the Apache Indians as follows:

May, 1869, they took from witness four horses and two mules; October, 1869, thirteen head of stock cattle; March, 1870, fifteen head of stock cattle—making a total loss amounting to $1,100; and believing that the Indians would take all he had, and probably his life, abandoned the Territory and moved to Sonora, in the Republic of Mexico. Considers the highways and fields unsafe for travel, or for men to operate in.

Antonio Grijalba, *sworn,* and says he is a farmer, and native of Tucson. On April 7th, 1870, the Apache Indians took from his corral twenty-seven head of cattle; that there is no security for life or property, either on the roads or in the fields, on account of the hostility of the Indians.

A. C. Ashton, *sworn:* Is a farmer and resides on the Santa Cruz River, in Pima County, and testifies to depredations by Apache Indians, as follows, to-wit:

In April, 1870, a band of friendly Papago Indians were attacked by Apaches, about three miles from his farm; one was killed and several horses were taken.

In May, 1870, nine men were attacked about seven miles above his farm; three were killed and one wounded.

May 20th, 1870, witness had stolen by them three animals valued at $600.

July 4th, 1870, a man and horse were killed and a mule and horse stolen, about five miles above his place.

In May, 1870, Reese Smith and Francisco Madrid were attacked near his farm, and lost two oxen.

July 12th, 1870, John Blanchard, keeping a grocery store near witness' place, had his store pillaged and lost everything by the Indians.

January 19th, 1871, Joseph King, who lived six miles below witness, was shot in the groin and lost four horses.

Considers the country insecure, on account of hostility of the Apache Indians.

Leopolde Carrillio, *sworn,* and says he is a merchant; resides in Tucson; is also a farmer. In August, 1869, had stolen from his farm at Punta de Agua, ten miles from Tucson, twenty-seven head of cattle. In November, 1869, three horses from the same farm. In March, 1870, twelve head of cattle. In April, 1870, from the Rietta, five miles from Tucson, five horses. From October, 1870, until this date, the Apaches have stolen at various times twenty head of cattle and one horse.

My total loss by Indians since August, 1869, amounts to about $2,000. All of the foregoing depredations were committed by hostile Apache Indians.

JOSE HERRERAS, *sworn:* Is a farmer and native of Arizona Territory. Testifies to depredations by Apache Indians as follows, to-wit:

In November, 1869, a man named Janero was killed by Indians, while in his employ; also saw the bodies of Juan Saiz and Angel Ortiga, after they were killed by Indians.

That at various times during the last two years he has lost about sixty-six head of cattle, of the value of $1,500.

Considers the Apache Indians more bold and hostile than ever before.

In May, 1870, they stole his horse and saddle from in front of his door; also that there is no safety for life or property in this Territory.

MATTIAS ROMERO, *sworn:* Is a farmer and native of this Territory. Testifies to the killing of Juan Saize by Indians (Apaches). Also saw two Mexicans, four miles southwest of Tucson, after they had been killed by Indians. These murders were committed in the spring of 1870. In November, 1869, saw two men who had been murdered by the Indians near the boundary line of Sonora. January, 1870, the Indians stole from me two yoke of oxen; March, 1870, three horses; October, 1870, two horses, and from my yard in Tucson they took two horses in November, 1870. Considers the Indians more bold than ever, and no safety for life or property exists in this Territory.

ANTONIO SOSO, *sworn:* Is a farmer and a native of this Territory. Testifies to the murder of Juan Saize, and an attack upon himself and party, in November, 1869, in which two horses were killed and two men wounded, by Apache Indians. On the same day the Apaches stole from him and others, one hundred head of cattle—witness losing all he had. That the Apache Indians are more bold and daring than at any time heretofore. That there is no safety to travelers or laborers outside of town.

M. G. GAY, *sworn:* Is engaged in the stock business; that he has resided in this Territory since 1858, and has a stock farm eight miles from Tucson. His loss of stock by Apache Indians, since January 1st, 1869, is as follows:

January 1st, 1870, one horse and two milch cows; in March, 1870, three animals; in July, 1870, two animals; in October,

1870, fourteen head of cattle; in November, 1870, seven head of cattle—making a total loss of $740; that there is no safety of life or property in the Territory, except at some military camp where the Indians are fed and rested, and from whence they raid upon the unprotected settlements of the Territory.

JESUS MA. ELIAS, *sworn:* Is a farmer and native of Tucson; in June, 1869, he saw at the Cañon de Oro, forty miles north of Tucson, two men, after they had been murdered, stripped and horribly mutilated by Apache Indians; about thirty days later he saw the bodies of two men who had been murdered by Apaches, about one mile below Camp Grant.

Witness had stolen from him, by Apache Indians, nine miles south of Tucson, five oxen; in August, 1870, eighteen beef cattle; in December, 1870, three oxen, and in January, 1871, several head of cattle (number not yet ascertained).

Witness also states that he is familiar with the habits of the Indians of this Territory, and knows that all of the Apaches at the present time are stealing and murdering whenever an opportunity occurs; that there is no safety in houses, fields, or highways.

GEORGE WESLEY, *sworn:* Is a farmer; resides sixty miles east of Tucson, on the San Pedro River; that in July, 1869, Wm. Johnson was killed on his farm, while at work in the field; on the same day two other men, named McMurry and McDonnell, were murdered and their mules taken; on January 7th, 1870, Samuel Brown and John F. Sims were murdered about three miles from their house. All of these murders were committed in my immediate neighborhood, and was done by Apache Indians. The witness helped to bury all of the foregoing murdered men, and they were all mutilated in a horrible manner.

In July, 1869, the Apaches again made an attack on his farm, drove them all off, took four horses, robbed the house— making a total loss to witness of $1,500.

On account of the hostility of the Apaches, has been obliged to abandon his farm; that he recognized some of the Indians that made the attack upon him as Camp Goodwin Apaches, fed by the U. S. Government.

JOAQUIN TELLES, *sworn:* Is a farmer and native of Tucson. The Apache Indians stole from him, in the vicinity of Tucson, in August, 1869, four head of cattle, valued at $150; that constant watch has to be kept in houses, fields, and highways, to prevent being murdered by the Indians; that in fact the whole Territory is in a state of siege.

Francisco Gunez, *sworn:* Is a butcher, and has lived in Arizona eleven years. On the 10th day of May, 1870, had thirteen head of cattle stolen by Apache Indians, about five miles east of Tucson, valued at $650. That during the year 1870 the Apache Indians stole from him, in excess of the foregoing, at various times, ten head of cattle, worth $500. That life and property are insecure everywhere in the Territory.

Guadalupe Saiz, *sworn:* Is a widow; owns a stock rancho near Tucson, and is a native of this Territory.

In the year 1870 she had stolen, by Apache Indians, twenty-nine head of cattle, worth at least $500. That the Indians are more hostile now than ever within her recollection.

N. B. Apple, *sworn:* Is a freighter, and resides in Tucson; that in the years 1869 and 1870 had several animals stolen by the Apache Indians; that on the 18th December, 1870, his train, while in company with the train of Tully & Ochoa, was attacked by not less than sixty Apache Indians, nine miles east of the Cienega Station; the Indians killed one man, wounded two men, and captured thirty-seven head of work cattle, also one mule and three saddle horses. The value of the property taken was about $2,000.

In September, 1869, my wagonmaster and teamsters buried seven men at the "Nogelas," near the boundary line, that had been killed by the Apache Indians.

In April, 1870, the Apaches attacked his train at Croton Springs, Arizona, but were repulsed.

Considers the roads extremely dangerous. Officers of the U. S. army invariably have large escorts and travel safely.

James Lee, *sworn:* Has resided in Tucson since 1856. On October 10th, 1870, witness, with a party of four others, pursued the Apache Indians that had stolen stock; overtook and had a fight with them, and was obliged to retreat, after one of the party was severely wounded.

Witness is part owner in a valuable silver mine located near Tucson, but is prevented from working the same on account of the hostility of the Apache Indians.

Depredations have been more frequent by the Apaches in the last year than during his residence in the Territory.

Francisco Grijalba, *sworn:* Is a resident of this Territory; occupation, a packer. In the spring of 1869 a man by the name of Juan Llepes was murdered, near Camp Whipple; two weeks later a party of three men were attacked between Camp Whipple and Camp Lincoln, murdered, and their animals captured.

In November, 1869, two men were murdered between Williamson Valley and Prescott, and twelve mules captured.

In March, 1870, John Snyder was attacked. between Lynx Creek and Prescott, and severely wounded, and lost three animals; about an hour later A. G. Dunn lost twenty head of cattle within a quarter of a mile of Prescott.

In August, 1870, two U. S. soldiers were attacked, near Walnut Grove, while they were carrying the U. S. mail; one was killed, one wounded, and the mail lost.

In October, 1870, a U. S. soldier and a citizen, in charge of the U. S. mail, were killed, and the horses and mail captured —all of the foregoing depredations were committed by the Apache Indians.

Witness says that he speaks the Apache language, and wa-informed by Apache Indians at Camp Thomas that the arms and ammunition issued by Col. Green to the so-called friendly Indians are loaned to other Indians who are deadly hostile to the whites, and that the Indians on the Camp Thomas Resers vation have numerous greenbacks, of the denomination of ten dollars up to fifty dollars, which they say were given them by "Penal Apaches" for powder and cotton cloth. The friendly Indians procure ammunition from the commanding officer, on pretense of hunting. and afterwards dispose of it to hostile Indians; that the friendly Indians are in the habit of leaving the reservation for the purpose of stealing stock on the line of Sonora, and the Indians at Camp Thomas only consider themselves at peace with the whites that live at that place. Witness states that he was captured by the Apache Indians when but twelve years of age, and lived with them four years, and has since been employed by the U. S. Government as a packer, guide, and interpreter.

A. J. LONG, *sworn:* Is a resident of this Territory, and by occupation a packer. When in the employ of the U. S. Government, at Camp Thomas, frequently saw "Miguil," one of the Apache chiefs, in possession of greenbacks, of denominations from twenty to fifty dollars; and the interpreter at said camp (Dodson) said he was in the habit of trading the Indians cartridges for turkeys. Witness considers all, or nearly all, of the tribe at the reservation hostile, and firmly believes that they leave the reservation at every favorable opportunity for the purpose of committing depredations.

JAMES SPEEDY, *sworn:* Is a mail rider, and lives in Tueson; while driving the U. S. mail stage from Tueson to Apache Pass, on the 15th of July, 1869, the stage was accompanied by a carriage containing three men; they were attacked by forty to fifty Apache Indians at Sulphur Springs. Witness with the mail coach escaped to Camp Bowie; troops were dispatched from the camp, and found one of the occupants of the carriage dead and all the property destroyed.

In September, 1869, the Apache Indians attacked fourteen men on the road from Tucson to Camp Grant, wounded one man, and had the entire party surrounded until relief reached them from Camp Grant.

JOHN H. FITZGERALD. *sworn:* Resides at Wickenburg, A. T.; is a member of the present Legislature; that the train of E. Ariola was attacked, five miles from the Vulture mine, by the Apache Indians, in the month of June, 1869, killing three men and capturing eighty mules, valued at $7,000.

In September, 1869, the Apaches attacked the men herding the mules of E. Ariola; they captured eighty-six mules and ten horses, while feeding in sight of the Vulture quartz mill.

In March, 1870, he went to the house of one McWilliams, on the river Hassayampa, and found Horace Greely, his partner, murdered by Indians and lying upon the floor.

In July, 1870, the Apache Indians took from Joseph Tyc and myself, while in camp near the town of Phœnix (Salt river), twelve head of work oxen; considers life and property unsafe in nearly all parts of the Territory.

A. LINN, *sworn:* Is a stock dealer; resides in Tucson. In October, 1869, two men, names unknown, were murdered by Apache Indians at the "Pecacho," on the road to Pima villages.

In December, 1869, the Apaches took from him fourteen head of cattle, at Blue Water Station. In October, 1870, seven head of cattle. In February, 1871, sixty head of cattle, from within nine miles of Tucson. Total value of losses by Apache Indians, $2,350. Considers the business of stock raising and farming very dangerous.

JOSE BUSTAMENTA, *sworn*, and says: The Apache Indians took from him, on the 2d day of February, 1871, in the suburbs of Tucson, one valuable horse. There is no security for life or property in the Territory at this time.

SABINO ORTERO, *sworn:* Is a farmer; resides at Tubac. In June, 1869, a boy in his employ was murdered by Apache Indians and five head of cattle taken; three months after they stole his horse; and in October, 1870, two boys employed by him were attacked by the Apache Indians, one of them murdered, and two horses taken.

About two weeks ago, Joseph King was wounded by them,

and lost four horses. Does not consider any portion of this country safe.

***

GABIANO ORTEGO, *sworn:* Is a farmer; resides in Pima county. In March, 1869, the Apache Indians captured from him, nine miles south of Tucson, twenty-five head of cattle, worth $400. In the month of April, 1870, they captured from him four head of cattle, worth $160. In June, 1870, four head of cattle, worth $150. Considers the Indians worse now than ever before.

***

TRANQUILINO VASQUES, *sworn:* On February 2d, 1871, the Apache Indians took from him, in the suburbs of Tucson, one horse; the Indians are worse now than for years before.

***

NIPOMOCENO BARAGAN, *sworn:* Is a native of New Mexico; a teamster. In December, 1870, while driving team for Tully & Ochoa, the train was attacked by Apache Indians; witness was wounded and is still disabled; Martin Rivera was killed; Theodosa Caravajal was wounded; and that the Indians making the attack had *good* firearms. There is no security for life or property—the Indians murder and plunder whenever opportunity offers.

***

M. G. GAY, *sworn:* On February 3d, 1871, the Apache Indians stole from his rancho, nine miles from Tucson, forty head of cattle, three sheep and two horses, valued at $1,100.

***

JUAN JOSE ORTIZ, *sworn:* On the 28th September, 1870, the Apache Indians murdered his son, twenty-six miles north of Tucson. In the year 1869 the same Indians stole from him one yoke of oxen, and in June, 1870, they stole one cow. There is no safety from the depredations of the Apache Indians in this Territory.

***

JOHN MILLER, *sworn:* Resides in Pima County. In July, 1869, the Apache Indians murdered a man by the name of Culver, while plowing in his field, and drove away his two horses. In September, 1869, they stole from a neighbor, named Hartzel, two horses. In October, 1869, they stole two horses from witness. All of which depredations were committed on the San Pedro River.

In May, 1870, they killed a United States soldier at the Cienega Station, and a cow belonging to witness, in sight of the station.

On July 9th, 1870, they attacked the Cienega Station and killed two men; and witness had to abandon the station on account of said hostilities. That said station is located on the southern overland mail road, twenty-five miles east of Tucson. Has lived in Arizona eight years, and has never known the Indians more hostile than now.

JESUS MARIA ORTIZ, *sworn:* Is a farmer, and native of this Territory. In April, 1869, the Apache Indians stole from him three work oxen; in May, 1869, one ox.

The Indians are more dangerous and hostile than ever before within his recollection. No farmer can with safety pursue his calling without having some one to watch the Indians.

HENRY GLASSMAN, *sworn:* Is a farmer and butcher, and testifies to the following depredations, committed by the Apache Indians, that have come under his personal observation:

On January 1st, 1869, Joaquin Tapia and James Catterson were murdered in the Sonoita Valley.

In June, 1869, witness lost by said Indians one cow, one calf, and two horses. About one week before this, his neighbor, Louis Quesse, had his entire herd, consisting of one hundred head of cattle, driven off by said Indians.

Considers the highways very unsafe for travelers.

WM. WRIGHT, *sworn:* Resides at the Potrero, seven miles north of the Sonora line. Testifies to the murder of several men during the year 1869 by the Apache Indians:

About the 15th May, 1870, three Mexicans were killed, and two wounded, five and a half miles from his place.

June 15th, the Indians killed a herder in the employ of Peter Kitchen, and took twelve head of oxen near his house.

June 17th, found the bodies of three men, near the boundary line, who had been murdered by Indians.

July 15th, the Indians made three attacks on his house, but were repulsed, capturing, however, one horse and one mule: knows that the horse last mentioned is in the hands of the Apache Indians at Camp Thomas.

SOLOMAN WARNER, *sworn:* Has resided in Tucson fourteen years; is a trader.

On the 29th of January, 1870, was attacked by Apache Indians; was wounded and crippled for life. There were seven men with him, of whom one was killed and one badly wounded. The Indians captured two horses and two mules and destroyed the ambulance and harness.

Considers the Apache Indians more hostile and dangerous now than since he has resided in the Territory.

H. W. Helling, *sworn:* His train was attacked by Apache Indians, January 18th, 1870, while *en route* from Florence to Camp McDowell. One man was murdered, two men wounded, eighteen mules captured, and the wagons and their contents totally destroyed. Loss to witness, $7,000.

Wm. J. O'Neil, *sworn:* Resides in Kirkland Valley, Yavapai County. In January, 1869, John T. Howell was attacked by fifty Indians, murdered, and two mules captured.

In July, 1869, four soldiers and one citizen, carrying the United States mail, between Prescott and Date Creek, were attacked by Indians. Two soldiers were killed and the citizen wounded, and the mail and five horses captured.

In November, 1869, Wesley White was killed by Indians while watching his corn crib, within fifty yards of his house.

In June, 1870, Alfred L. Johnson and "Kentuck" were murdered by Indians, about twelve miles above Camp Date Creek, on the road to Prescott.

Considers the Indians more hostile and dangerous now than since his residence in the Territory.

John W. Hopkins, *sworn:* Residence, Tucson; occupation, lumberman. Testifies to a number of murders by the Apache Indians during the years 1869 and 1870. Has passed over no road in the Territory upon the side of which there are not to be found numerous graves of victims, who have fallen at the hands of hostile Apache Indians, and considers the Apache Indians of this Territory in more active hostility than at any period since his residence in the Territory.

Wm. J. Ross, *sworn:* Is an officer in the United States army. That in March, 1870, the Apache Indians captured nineteen head of cattle near the rancho of Thomas Gardner, on the Sonoita River.

That in November, 1869, the Apache Indians stole some tents from within a few yards of the rear of the officers' quarters, at Camp Crittenden.

That, from authentic reports, he considers murders and depredations by Apache Indians of more frequent occurrence than at any time since his residence in the Territory, and that the roads and highways are very dangerous for small traveling parties.

John Rodgers, *sworn:* Resides in Pima County; occupation, farmer. That in the month of April, 1869, the Apache Indians captured, near the Nogelas, forty-six mules and one horse, of the estimated value of $4,700.

Also, at the same place, in the month of May, 1870, six men were attacked by said Indians, three of whom were killed and one wounded, and a considerable amount of stock captured.

Testifies to a number of other depredations committed on the Santa Cruz River during the years 1869, 1870, and 1871, by the Indians, and considers all business impaired in consequence of the hostility of the Apache Indians.

S. R. DeLong, *sworn:* Testifies that from the 1st of January, 1869, to the 31st of December, 1870, the firm of Tully & Ochoa lost by raids of the Apache Indians, in merchandise, wagons, horses, mules, oxen, and other property, to the value of $18,500.

Thos. Banning, *sworn:* Residence, Arizona; occupation, carpenter. That about January 19th, 1871, the Apache Indians captured from Milton Ward and José ———, on the Gila River, 90 miles north of Tucson, twenty-seven head of mules, of the estimated value of $1,000.

That about the 15th of January, 1871, the Apache Indians captured from D. C. Thompson, on the Gila River, eight animals.

John L. Taylor, *sworn:* Residence, Prescott, A. T.; was formerly Sheriff of Yavapai County; is at present a member of the Legislature; that in the fall of 1869, a man by the name of Osborn was murdered, about two miles north of Prescott, by Indians.

That in the fall of 1870 he assisted in burying the body of William Dennison; and that about two weeks thereafter Thomas Rutlidge was murdered, about two miles from Prescott, the Indians taking from him two horses and one pistol.

Considers the Apache Indians more hostile and bold at the present time than heretofore.

Ramon Pacheco, *sworn:* Is a native of Arizona; occupation, freighter. That in September, 1870, he saw, on the road to Camp Crittenden, the bodies of three men who had been murdered by Apache Indians.

That in the month of November, 1870, while hauling lumber from Santa Rita Mountains, the Apache Indians captured eight yoke of oxen, two mules, and one horse. All valued at $1,500.

That there is no security for life or property on the roads, or outside of the towns.

Alphonso Rickman, *sworn:* Occupation, farmer. That the

Apache Indians attacked his train, in the month of February. killing one man and capturing sixteen mules. Witness followed the Indians and recaptured twelve of the mules.

That during the last eighteen months he has resided sixty miles south of Tucson, on the Sonoita River, and since his residence there the Apache Indians have constantly committed depredations and murders. That there is absolutely no safety either in the fields, on the roads, or in the vicinity of military posts and towns.

JOSEPH MELVIN, *sworn:* Residence near Camp Verde, Yavapai County. Is at present a member of the Legislature.

That early in the year 1869 witness and J. J. Gibson were attacked by seventy-five Indians, at Ash Creek. Gibson was mortally wounded and his gun captured, and about $150 worth of property was captured from witness. That soon after the last mentioned attack, the Indians attacked two citizens and one soldier near "Grief Hill," killing the soldier, mortally wounding one citizen, and capturing one mule and two pistols.

Considers the Indians more hostile than at any time heretofore.

LOUIS QUESSE, *sworn:* Has resided in Arizona fourteen years; occupation, blacksmith. That in January, 1869, the Apache Indians captured from his rancho, near Tubac, two horses and eight head of cattle. That about January 30th, 1869, the same Indians killed four head belonging to witness. That about the 27th of February, 1869, the same Indians attacked his cattle corral, wounding two Papago Indians and capturing thirty-three head of cattle. That August 15th, 1869, the same Indians captured eight horses and two mules from his rancho. That in the month of October, 1869, the same Indians captured nine head of cattle. That in January, 1870, the same Indians captured eleven head of cattle. That in April, 1870, they captured four head of cattle. That in October, 1870, they attacked his herder, wounding him severely, capturing one horse, one gun, and fifteen head of cattle. That February 6th, 1870, they killed four head of cattle near his house. That his total loss by Apache Indians, during the years 1869 and 1870, amounts to $3,655.

That in the town of Tubac the citizens are afraid to appear on the streets after dark, on account of Indians.

JAMES PETERS, *sworn:* Residence, Tucson; occupation, teamster. That in June, 1870, witness assisted in burying David Holland, who was murdered by the Apache Indians, on the farm of T. M. Yerkes, while at work in the field.

That in September, 1870, the Apache Indians captured from witness, on the road between Camp Crittenden and the Santa Rita Sawmill, eight yoke of oxen, of the value of $800.

That, of his own knowledge, several murders were committed by the Indians during the year 1870, and considers the Indians more hostile now than they have ever been.

JOHN HAMMELL, *sworn:* Residence, Pima County; occupation, teamster. That, February 2d, 1870, while employed in driving a Government team between Tucson and Pima villages, at a point thirteen miles north of the Point of Mountain, he was attacked by forty or fifty Apache Indians; that there were four teams in the party; that the Indians killed two men and mortally wounded two, and captured twenty mules ; that there was an escort of six men, who, at the time of the attack, were ahead of the wagons about five hundred yards and did not come to our assistance.

W. H. SIMPSON, *sworn:* Residence, Pima County; occupation, miner. That in December, 1870, the Apache Indians captured from Mendia & Trujillo, within three miles of Tucson, sixteen mules. That the Indians have committed more depredations in the past three months than for six months previous.

SANTA CRUZ CASTANIDA, *sworn:* Is a native of New Mexico; occupation, teamster. That in May, 1869, while in the employ of Tully & Ochoa, and acting as wagonmaster of their train, he was attacked, on the road to Camp Grant, by a large band of Apache Indians; that there were nine wagons and fourteen men belonging to the train ; that the Apaches commenced the attack at 8 o'clock, A. M.; that he brought the wagons together and fought the Indians until near sundown ; that he had a small howitzer which he used in the action ; that near sundown his ammunition gave out, and the entire party would have been murdered but for the arrival of some troops from Camp Grant; that they were all obliged to retreat, with the loss of the entire train, and leaving the bodies of three men ; that there were ten mules killed in the action, and the balance were driven off by the Indians.

That, on the 18th day of December, 1870, the Apache Indians attacked a train of nine wagons, belonging to Tully & Ochoa, and of which he was in charge, twenty-nine miles east of Tucson, on the road to Camp Goodwin; that one man was killed, two wounded, and thirty-nine yoke of oxen and three horses captured.

Witness further states, that in the fight he had with the Indians, in May, 1869, he saw and talked with an Indian named " Cisco ;" and that said Indian lived at Camp Goodwin, and was fed and protected by the Government. And witness further states that the Indians are now more hostile than at any time heretofore.

EUGENE EDMUNDS, *sworn :* Residence, Pima County ; occupation, freighter; that in October, 1870, the Apache Indians captured from him nine animals, of the value of $850; that of his own knowledge, several murders were committed by Indians during the year 1870.

GUILLERMO TELLES, *sworn :* Is a native of Arizona; occupation, farmer; owns a farm, three miles south of Tucson, and has lived there for sixty years; that in the month of September, 1869, the Apache Indians stole from him seven cows, and in November, 1870, eleven head of cattle—total value of all being $600; that he has never known the Indians so hostile and dangerous as at the present time; that there is no security for life and property in the Territory.

FRED L. AUSTIN, *sworn :* Occupation, merchant; that about the 30th of September, 1869, he and a party of twelve others were attacked by about one hundred and fifty Apache Indians, on the road from Tucson to Camp Grant; that they fought the Indians from 9 o'clock A. M. until 4 o'clock P. M., when relief came from Camp Grant; that he has resided at Camp Grant for the last eighteen months, during which time the Apache Indians have been very hostile, committing murders and depredations on travelers and farmers.

II. C. HOOKER, *sworn :* Residence, Pima County; is one of the firm of Hinds & Hooker; that in 1869, at Sacaton Cattle Camp, his herder was killed and forty head of cattle taken by the Apache Indians ; that in the year 1870, the Indians took four horses and thirteen head of cattle belonging to said firm, at Camp Grant, and also one horse at Camp McDowell; that in the same year, at Williamson Valley, near Camp Rawlins, one man in the employ of said firm was killed, three horses, two mules and three hundred sheep captured; at Camp Thomas, in the same year, fourteen head of beef cattle were stolen by the so-called friendly Indians at that Post; that at Camp Bowie, in the same year, two horses were stolen ; that at the Fresnal Rancho, during the years 1869 and 1870, the said firm lost by the Apache Indians over four hundred head of cattle—estimated loss of which is $18,000.

THOMAS EWING, *sworn :* Residence, Tucson ; occupation, contractor. That he is now supplying the United States Government with grain, as follows: At Camp Lowell, $3.30, coin, per 100 pounds; at Camp Bowie, $5.35, coin, per 100 pounds; at Camp Grant, $4.37½, coin, per 100 pounds; at Camp Goodwin, $5.85, coin, per 100 pounds. That he pays at Tucson, in currency, $3.50 per 100 pounds for barley, and $2.50 to $3 per 100 pounds for corn; that good flour can be purchased for $5 per 100 pounds, and hay at $15 per ton.

FREDERICK GROHE, *sworn:* Residence, Tucson; occupation, teamster. That in 1870 a train, with which he was employed as teamster, was attacked by Apache Indians, and two men were killed and two wounded. That the Apache Indians are more hostile than heretofore.

SAMUEL B. WISE, *sworn:* Occupation, farmer, Has resided in the Territory fifteen years. That in December, 1869, he and others had taken, by the Apache Indians, near Camp Crittenden, fifty-one head of animals.

That in February, 1870, the Apache Indians broke into the corral, at Blue Water Station, belonging to witness, and stole two horses and one mule. And, within his knowledge, he knows of no road in the Territory that is safe for travelers.

HIRAM S. STEVENS, *sworn:* Residence, Tucson; occupation, merchant. That, of his own knowledge, several murders have been committed by Indians.

That he was with Capt. Moulton, First United States Cavalry, who had an engagement with the Indians; that Capt. Moulton had twenty men with him, but had to retreat, after having two men and five horses wounded.

JOHN T. SMITH, *sworn:* Residence, eight miles south of Tubac; occupation, farmer. That, in May, 1869, the Apache Indians took from the rancho where he was stopping one hundred and thirty head of cattle; that he, with eighteen others, pursued the Indians, and recaptured most of the cattle, but were afterward driven out of the mountains by the Indians. That, of his own knowledge, several murders have been committed in the Dragoon Mountains, and in the Santa Cruz Valley.

CONRADO AGUIRRE, *sworn:* Residence, Tucson; occupation, freighter. Testifies that his train was captured in 1869 by the Apache Indians, at the Nogelas, and seven men murdered, and total value of property taken, $5,000. That a few days later, near the same place, a train was captured by the Indians, and three men and one woman murdered.

That in January, 1870, witness and four others were attacked by sixty Apache Indians, near Sasabi Flat, on the road from Tucson to Altar, and the whole party murdered except himself. That among the murdered men were his brother and brother-in-law.

Witness estimates his loss at $3,000.

———

R. F. BERNARD, *sworn:* Is a captain in the 1st U. S. Cavalry; testifies that in October, 1869, witness, with thirteen men, followed a band of Apache Indians that had taken a train on the road from Tucson to Camp Grant, and overtook the Indians in Arivipa Mountains, but finding them about three hundred strong was obliged to retreat. That in July, 1869, the Indians broke into a house at Camp Bowie; and about the same time attacked the mail rider one and a half miles from the same Post, killing his horse and capturing the mail; that a short time afterward a party of men were attacked and six horses captured; that about the same time, sixty miles east of Camp Bowie, two mail wagons were attacked and four men killed, and all the animals and property captured. That in October, 1869, the mail coach was attacked at Dragoon Springs, stage driver and all the passengers killed, and the mail and animals captured; that about the same time, and near the same place, a party of men were attacked, and one man killed and one wounded, and three hundred head of cattle captured. That on November 11th, 1869, the Government herd was taken at Camp Bowie. That in December, 1869, the Indians captured twenty-five mules belonging to a train within one-half mile of the Post; and about the same time attacked two wagons at Sulphur Springs and killed five mules; that in the latter part of December they killed two men, near the San Pedro Station, and in the same month captured nineteen horses and mules belonging to the Government, that were tied outside of the corral at Camp Bowie; that in January, 1870, they captured thirteen animals at the same Post; that in the summer of 1870 they shot a man with two arrows as he stepped out of his house. Also testifies to many other depredations committed near Camp Bowie during his residence at that post; that he considers the Indians more hostile and dangerous than he ever knew them, and does not consider the roads safe for travelers without an escort.

———

HUGH L. HINDS, *sworn:* Testifies that he is a trader by occupation, and has resided in the Territory nine years; has been in business at Camp Goodwin, and during his residence at said Post, the Apache Indians that were fed and protected at said Post by the Government, robbed him of stock, and frequently came into the Post with stolen property and stock; that in January, 1869, the Apache Indians stole from him, on the Rio Grande, two hundred head of cattle; same year, at Barney's Station, eight mules, valued at $1,000; also at the San Cimon, near Gila River, in 1870, sixteen mules, valued at $2,000; also at Camp Goodwin, in 1870, fourteen head of horses and mules, valued at $1,700; in same year, at Camp McDowell, twelve head, and at Camp Thomas, sixteen head of cattle; that one man in his employ was killed at Camp Goodwin, and another at Sacaton; also knows of a train being captured between Wickenburg and Salt River, in January, 1871; also of two trains losing all their animals at the same time, and near the same place; also knows of a loss during said month of sixteen head of animals, at the Gila settlements, and the capture of a train belonging to Hellings & Co., valued at $6,000; that he never knew the Indians to be as bad as they are at the present time.

ABRAHAM LYONS, *sworn:* Testifies that he has lived in the Territory since 1857, and is a freighter by occupation; that he has traveled extensively over the Territory, and has witnessed many depredations and murders that have been committed by the Apache Indians; and that murders and robberies have been of more frequent occurrence during the last two years than heretofore since his residence in the Territory; that he formerly traveled through the country with four or five men, and now deems it unsafe to travel without twelve or fifteen men.

ALPHONZO LAZARD, *sworn:* Testifies that he has lived thirteen years in the Territory, and is by occupation a trader; that the Apache Indians captured from him, during the year 1869, forty-nine head of animals, valued at $4,800; that during the year 1870, the Apache Indians captured from him sixty-three head of animals and goods, of the total value of $5,000; and that in January, 1871, the Indians took three head of oxen from him, of the value of $125.

WM. J. OSBORN, *sworn:* Testifies that on the 2d of February, 1870, the Apache Indians captured from him four mules, of the value of $600; that he has resided in the Territory during the last eight years, and that the Apache Indians have been more active in their hostilities, and have committed more depredations and murders within the last two years than at any other time during his residence in the Territory.

A. P. K. SAFFORD, *sworn,* and says he is the present Governor of the Territory, and has traveled extensively through the same, and does not consider that any portion of it is safe from depredations by the Apache Indians, except along and a few miles east of the Colorado River; and since his residence there is scarcely a road or trail east of that point that has not been the scene of Indian hostilities; that at this time scarcely a day passes without murders and robberies being reported to him; and that he has never known the Indians more active and successful than now; that the Apache Indians depend principally for their support upon theft and robbery, and do not desire nor will they accept any terms of peace until they are thoroughly subjugated by military power; that they are cruel in the extreme, witness having seen, in August, the charred remains of a white man who had evidently been burned alive—also a scalp, tied to a pole; that the country possesses abundant resources for a large and prosperous population; that the climate is mild and salubrious; that for grazing it is unsurpassed, and all kinds of cereals and vegetables are produced in abundance; that good coal in quantities has been found—also an abundance of salt; and that in nearly every mountain is found mines of gold, silver, copper, and lead; that wheat, barley, and corn can be purchased at two and one-half cents per pound, and very little sold at that price.

D. C. THOMPSON, *sworn:* Testifies that he resides on the Gila River, in Pima County; that in January, 1870, the Apaches attacked his herd of cattle and captured ninety-one head; that in the same month they attacked a train of five wagons, on the road to Camp McDowell, and killed the owner of the train, named Santiago Campilla, captured forty-eight work oxen and destroyed all the property with the train; that in February they attacked a wagon train, fifteen miles from Adamsville, killed one man and captured all the animals.

JAMES A. MOORE, *sworn:* Testifies that from April, 1869, to the 14th of April, 1870, the Apache Indians have captured from his station, forty-one head of cattle and seven horses.

H. MORGAN, *sworn:* Testifies that since the 1st of December, 1870, to February 14th, 1871, the Apache Indians have made five raids on the Pima and Maricopa Indian Reservation, and captured twenty-nine head of cattle.

JOHN T. ALSOP, *sworn:* Testifies that he resides at Phœnix, Maricopa County; is a farmer, and a member of the present Legislature. That there is in the County of Maricopa fifty thousand acres of good arable land, suitable for agriculture, most of which lies in one body, known as the "Phœnix Settlement;" that said location is very healthy; that there is now under cultivation five or six thousand acres; that the usual average yield per acre is forty bushels; that all kinds of vegetables produce well; that experiments in cultivating fruit trees indicate excellent soil and climate for the same.

MILTON WARD, *sworn*, and says that he is a farmer, and resides near Adamsville, Pima County, Arizona Territory. That on the 12th day of January, 1869, the Apache Indians captured, from his residence, twenty-three head of cattle, worth $815, and on the 22d day of February, one yoke of oxen, worth $100; and on the 14th day of January, 1871, they captured from the same place twelve head of mules and one horse, worth $1,560; making a total loss to the witness, during the past two years, by said Indians, of $2,475.

SABERIANO ORTIZ, *sworn*, and says: That he is a farmer, and resides on the Gila River, six miles below Adamsville. That the Apache Indians captured from him, on the 12th day of January, 1869, three animals, worth $140; and on the 10th day of February following, six horses, worth $360; and on the 12th day of December, 1870, three horses, worth $200; making a total loss to witness, during the past two years, by said Indians, of $700.

MARTIN VAROLAS, *sworn*, and says that he is a farmer and resides near Adamsville, Pima County, A. T.; that the Apache Indians captured from him, on the 20th day of June, 1870, one horse, worth $70, and on the 10th day of June, a horse worth $100; and on the 15th day of August following, while *en route* to Wickenburg, one mule, worth $100—making a total loss to witness, by said Indians, during the past two years, of $270.

JESUS GONZALES, *sworn*, and says that on or about the 11th day of February, 1870, the Apache Indians captured from him, at the Casa Grande Settlement, on the Gila River, two mules and two horses, worth $350; and at the Salt River Settlements, on or about the 22d day of December, 1870, one ox, worth $40; and on the 14th day of January, 1871, they captured from him, three miles below Adamsville, four mules, worth $400—making a total loss to witness, during the past two years, by said Indians, of $790.

TEODORO PESQUEIRA, *sworn*, and says that he resides near Adamsville, Pima County, A. T.; that on the 1st day of September, 1869, the Apache Indians captured from him one horse, worth $100; and that he was attacked by said Indians, on the road between Tucson and the Picacho, on the 27th day of September, 1869, and had one horse killed, worth $400; and on the 15th day of December, 1870, they captured one ox from his residence near Adamsville, worth $40.

J. R. CHAMBERS, *sworn*, and says that on the 25th day of November, 1869, the Apache Indians attacked James Hollister, six miles above Florence, on the Gila River, and mortally wounded him, from the effects of which he died, two days afterward.

ANTONIO CONTRARAS, *sworn*, and says that the Apache Indians captured from him, on the 20th of May, 1869, at the old mill, above Tucson, seven mules, worth $800.

NASARIO ORTIZ, *sworn*, and says that the Apache Indians captured from him, on the 28th day of February, 1869, at White's Rancho, two miles below Adamsville, twenty head of oxen, worth $800; and on the 28th day of October, 1869, they captured from his train, while *en route* from the Gila River to Camp McDowell, three oxen, worth $120; and on the 2d day of January, 1870, while on the above referred to road, they captured from his train six mules, worth $400; and on the 15th day of January, same year, they captured, from his residence near Adamsville, one mule and one horse, worth $150— making a total loss to the witness, during the past two years, of $1,470.

The undersigned hereby certify that the annexed and foregoing is a correct and true digest of the testimony taken by the Joint Special Committee of the Legislative Assembly of the Territory of Arizona, appointed to take such testimony, concerning depredations on property and murders committed by the Apaches and hostile Indians, in this Territory, and reported to the Legislative Assembly of said Territory on the 17th day of February, A. D. 1871.

Attest: M. D. DOBBINS,
    J. E. McCAFFRY,   *Speaker of the House of Representatives.*
       Chief Cl'k H. of R.

Attest: HARTLEY H. CARTER,
    JNO. ANDERSON,   *President of the Council.*
      Sec'y of the Council.